FRIENDS

AND

LOTS OF FUDGE

FRIENDS AND LOTS OF FUDGE

Amy Barnett

Illustrated by Gill Jones

First published in Great Britain in 2024

Copyright © Amy Barnett 2024

The right of Amy Barnett to be identified as the author and of this work had been asserted by her in accordance with the Copyright, Designs and Patents Act 1988. All rights reserved. No part of this publication may be reproduced transmitted or stored in a retrieval system, in any form or by any means, without permission in writing from the author, nor be otherwise circulated in any form of binding or cover other than that in which it is published and without a similar condition being imposed on the subsequent purchaser. All characters in this publication are fictitious and any resemblance to real people, alive or dead, is purely coincidental.

Published by Amazon

Chapter 1
The Meeting

Ring, ring. Megan jerked awake, frantically rubbing her dark blue eyes and leaping out of bed, slamming on her glasses as she did so. Her wavy hair went flying as she dashed to the closet, wrenched open the door and grabbed her green and white school uniform. 'Today's the day' she thought, as she pulled on her trousers. 'The day I finally make a friend'.

She had been waiting with anticipation until she would make a friend. There was something about today's bright, sunny day that projected a feeling of hope in the air. Practically flying down the rickety stairs, she emerged like a whirlwind into the kitchen, where her dad was attempting to make pancakes. Unfortunately, he was failing dismally.

"Wow! What's got you so cheerful?" questioned Dad, throwing away yet another burnt pancake.

Her mother was settled on the sofa, reading the day's edition of Beautiful Beauty, as usual. She was wearing her favourite high-heeled shoes. Megan shrugged in answer to her dad's question and then gulped down some breakfast, sweeping her long hair behind her shoulders beforehand.

Megan skipped to school, which was only a few blocks away. Worthing Road was a very convenient place to live, with houses that looked exactly the same from a distance but from close up surprisingly different.

Her day had started off great, but what Megan didn't know was that it was about to take an unexpected turn.

As she entered the gates, she heard a terrible sound that made her heart skip a beat. Raucous gales of laughter split the still air and, not for the first time, she wished she could disappear.

Panic rose inside her like an angry snake. She was wearing her pink unicorn slippers!! She hadn't really registered the stares she was attracting as she walked down the street, but now she realised why.

She was desperately trying to master the impulse not to cry. Unable to bear it any longer, she dashed sobbing into the girls' toilets and locked herself in the nearest cubicle.

She could not believe that she had woken up really happy but now all she could do was cry. The laughter was still ringing in her ears like her alarm clock. Sitting down on the toilet she let the tears cascade down her red cheeks and into her mouth. That bitter taste. She hated that taste.

Suddenly she heard tapping on the graffitied, rusty cubicle door. Megan stayed quiet, desperately trying to hide her fluffy slippers behind the toilet. Someone was tapping on the door, calling to her.

"Hello."

This voice was a girl's voice, and friendlier than any she had heard before in St Brutus' School. Hesitantly, she opened the cubicle door. It creaked loudly. On the threshold stood a girl Megan's own age with long, black, straight hair, green eyes and thick black eyebrows.

"My name is Emma," she stammered, clearly just as scared as Megan was herself.

"Megan," replied Megan.

"I don't think those are school shoes…." said the girl, gesturing at the childish slippers.

"Like I haven't noticed!" answered Megan, sarcastically.

"Sorry, it's just, well, I've seen you all alone on the bench every break, and… I haven't got a friend either." blurted out Emma.

"Join the club" said Megan, bitterly.

She saw a tear well up in Emma's eye and trickle slowly down her face.

Emma blinked them back bravely and said shakily, "That's the bell. We had better go inside."

"OK," said Megan, reluctantly.

"You can borrow my PE shoes if you want. They're not school shoes, but they'll do."

"Thanks," said Megan, taking the bag containing the hand-me-down shoes and putting them on gratefully. Suddenly, she noticed Emma's hands were covered in cuts and scratches.

When Emma saw Megan looking at her hands, she quickly withdrew them and started to trudge towards the classroom. With her mind clouded with horrible possibilities of how the scratches had got there, Megan followed Emma into class.

Chapter 2
Hope

When Megan got home that day she found, to her very great surprise, her Grandpa was waiting for her in the small, cosy living-room.

"Grandpa! What are you doing here?"

"To see you, of course!" replied Grandpa, in his usual gruff but kind voice. He had grey hair and a curly moustache. He was wearing old glasses and a blue raincoat.

Megan would usually be overjoyed to see her Grandpa but considering the awful day she had had, even seeing him could not lighten her present darkness.

Mrs. Spite, their form mistress, had given them a pile of homework in Maths, English, Geography and French; none of which Megan understood.

Grandpa must have seen the look

on her face, because he asked, "Are you alright, Megan, dear?" He sounded concerned.

"Yes, yes, just surprised that is all."

He didn't seem satisfied with her response.

Her dad came in moodily, sitting down on the sofa and grabbed a biscuit from the box sitting on the messy coffee table. It had been another frustrating day trying to find a job, with no success.

Her mother was yet again slumped on the armchair pouring over her beauty magazine, ignoring the goings on.

Megan was burning to tell her Grandpa what had happened, but her throat constricted and suddenly she could not speak. She felt her face grow hot. To cover up these suspicious signs, she grabbed a biscuit and excused herself to go upstairs. When there, she paced the room, going through the horror of the slipper episode in her head, wishing she could simply cast it away.

She was thinking about that girl she had met. Was there still hope that she would find a trustworthy, loving and happy friend? Could this small, meek girl be the friend she'd been waiting for, for so long, the one who would make school not only bearable but positively fun? How Megan hoped she might.

Suddenly, she saw something out of her grimy bedroom window. It was a girl. Not just any girl. This was Emma, the girl who had talked to her at school. The girl with long straight hair and shy, pitiful eyes. Megan stopped pacing at once and dashed over to her window, shocked.

What made her surprise increase was when the girl turned into Megan's gravelled driveway. Her heart was pounding against her chest madly. As she knew it would, the doorbell rang, shrilly. She heard her father jump and knock over one of her mother's fancy china ornaments. Cursing, her dad got up reluctantly and stamped to the door. He wrenched the door open quite unnecessarily. The girl looked positively alarmed when the door flew open. As her dad saw this poor, bedraggled girl on the threshold, his anger seeped silently away as fast as it had come.

"Um. Please may I see Megan?" stammered the girl shaking from her head to her battered shoes. A look of polite bewilderment spread over Megan's dad's face but he didn't say anything. Tongue-tied, he simply pointed upstairs.

Chapter 3
A New Friend

Megan stood stock still, facing her closed bedroom door, which had a poster of her favourite football team pinned to it. She could not believe it. Emma had actually come to see her, Megan Greenway. Amid all the shock, there was a bright ray of hope and with that came the urge to make sure this timid girl became her friend... Her friend for life.

Meanwhile, Emma stood frozen in the act of reaching for Megan's rusty door-handle. Tentatively, as though something sinister lurked behind, Emma pushed the door ajar and said, not concealing the note of panic in her voice, "Hello."

Megan stood stationary, staring at the new arrival, her face completely blank, and unable to think what to do or indeed what to say. Finally, she decided a simple hello was good enough.

"Hello."

There was an awkward silence as Megan cast around for something to say. Emma broke the silence.

"If you're wondering how I knew where you lived, I saw you out of my window because I've just moved in across the street and started at St Brutus'."

Megan opened her mouth, stupidly, then closed it again, at a loss for what to say.

"So, why don't you have any friends? You seem very nice to me."

Megan was so surprised that Emma had sprung that question on her just like that that she didn't answer immediately. Emma didn't seem to find this odd. She simply fiddled idly with a hole in her jumper.

Megan knew Emma was pretending not to listen, so replied solemnly, "It just hasn't been possible."

It was Emma's turn to look surprised. "Come again?"

"It just hasn't been possible." She said again, a little impatiently this time.

"I don't understand." Said Emma, curiously.

"Well, I was ill when I was young and it meant I couldn't go to school 'til I was eight, so everyone thought I was stupid because I'd missed so much work."

"I'm sorry." Emma replied, kindly.

'St Brutus' was the only school with space, and as you've seen, it isn't a very nice school. None of the teachers are interested in teaching, they just hang around the staff room gossiping and spreading lies about the pupils, and then they set us lots of homework. They don't even feed us proper meals! Ofsted hasn't come for years, so nobody's noticed!"

"That doesn't sound good." said Emma, quietly.

"I've tried to make friends with some of the girls but they've all got their own friends by now and they can't be bothered to get to know me."

Megan stared out of the window, feeling that she'd said too much.

After a while, Megan spoke up again, "I have been meaning to ask you... um..." She wasn't sure how to put this personal question.

Emma waited expectantly.

"Why... Why have you got, you know, scratches on your hands?" Megan asked, apprehensively.

Emma hesitated. This was clearly a hard subject for her.

"Well," she said, "it's a bit of a story..."

"Go on," said Megan, not wanting to sound nosey, but eager to hear more all the same.

Emma still looked hesitant but seeing Megan's curious but reassuring face, she relented.

"I...." she began, nervously. "I got cornered in an alleyway on my home from school yesterday. A... A gang of bullies pinned me against a nearby sharp-edged wall and..." she seemed unable to continue, as though the memory of it caused her considerable pain.

"And they… they scratched my hands with the edge of the wall, and that's why I've got scratches" she finished, shortly.

Megan was too appalled to speak. She tried to say sorry, but all that came out of her mouth was a strange gurgling noise. Emma bowed her head. She seemed to understand Megan's odd noise.

Megan, out of respect for her feelings, stayed silent, thinking desperately for something, anything, to say that would alleviate at least some of her new friend's pain.

When Emma lifted her head up, Megan saw that her eyes were slightly bloodshot and her complexion pale grey. Megan felt so sorry for Emma and the horrid life she seemed to lead that she decided to cheer her up if she could. Luckily, she knew just the place. The sweet shop!

Chapter 4
The Sweet Shop

Megan and Emma were on their way to the sweetshop wearing their large winter coats, which were flowing back behind them in the strong wind. Emma's face was still tinged with grey and both of their heads were bowed against what was becoming a gale. The rain was lashing against their faces like the bite of a leopard, hunting its prey.

"Is this really necessary?" yelled Emma, through the howling of the wind.

"You'll see." Megan shouted back.

Emma groaned. Evidently she hated rain.

"Here we are," cried Megan. "Follow me!"

They had turned into a shop so colourful that both had to blink rapidly to make out the towering shelves of sherbet lemons, jelly beans, caramel eggs, cream eggs, dark chocolate, white chocolate and mounds upon mounds of fudge; all different colours and flavours. Megan, with a look of mild pride on her face, began to examine the latest fudge:

POWERFUL PEPPERMINT: PUNCHY AND UNDOUBTEDLY PERFECT.

Emma was still staring, open-mouthed, at the scene before her. Slowly it began to dawn on her that she was not dreaming, and that this was all unmistakably genuine. Realising that she was blocking the entrance, she joined Megan and instantly became mesmerised by the glittering deliciousness of a world like no other.

Megan had succeeded. Emma was happy! Hopefully it would last!

Munching noisily on their sweets (which had taken at least an hour to choose!), the girls were once again in Megan's cluttered room

"Wow!" cried Emma, as she bit into a chocolate flavoured fudge. "I never knew fudge was so delicious!"

Megan, who had just bitten into a jelly-bean, spat it out in amazement. "You have never tried one!" cried Megan, in total disbelief.

"No, I've never been allowed one, or, well…. I never had enough money to."

Megan, who had fudge nearly every day and could not imagine a world without it, felt again the inescapable pity for her friend.

Emma's face had gone pink as though she had said too much, and she was suddenly oddly interested in her sweets.

There was a silence.

Then Emma said that she should probably get home or her mother would worry.

"OK" said Megan. She loved being with her friend but she was exhausted and felt that she could do with an early night.

She watched as Emma opened her door, descended the stairs and gently closed the front door behind her.

Megan snuggled into bed, but despite the warm memories of the day, she couldn't help feeling a little uneasy.

Chapter 5
Time to Face School

Ring, ring, went Megan's alarm clock. This time she did not leap out of bed but flopped onto the floor with a low moan. She had had the worst night and wished she could keep sleeping for she knew she would need her wits about her. If the bullies who'd hurt Emma's hands found out that Emma had a friend, they would surely target her as well.

She heaved herself up and groped for her glasses. Without them she couldn't even see past the end of her nose. She slouched downstairs, nearly tripping over her own feet. She now felt faintly sick.

Megan tried to force down food but her throat had stopped working and her head was pounding.

Emma was waiting for her at the school gates but she wasn't alone. Two muscular, brutal looking figures flanked her, each grasping one of her arms.

"Aha. Here's the other worm." Said the toughest of the two, with a nasty grin that looked more like a leer. He was wearing baggy jeans with rips everywhere and a large t shirt with a skull on it. Megan froze. She knew she had no chance to rescue her friend without help from others, but who would help her? She was the girl with the unicorn slippers.

"Come on, Bruce. Let's do it" said one of them punching his fist into his hand, an evil gleam in his eye.

"Do what, exactly?" said Megan, more bravely than she felt.

"Oh, you'll find out soon enough" sneered Bruce.

The other grunted in apparent amusement at his companion's statement.

They shoved Emma to the ground, where she lay motionless, and then they lunged at Megan who, caught unawares, was thrown down as well, feeling her head thud against the ground and a lump rising rapidly on it. Face down on the gravel she heard, as though from a great distance, a voice shouting: "How dare you!" Almost blinded from the throbbing pain, she raised her head just enough to see a woman who looked strangely familiar charging towards the bullies. The last thing Megan saw before her eyes closed was a high heeled shoe flying through the air and hitting one of the bullies squarely in the face. Her head slumped onto the ground as she fainted.

Chapter 6
The Hospital

Megan's body was aching and her heart was racing. She could hear voices coming from nearby saying things she was too tired to understand.

"What a terrible business," said someone, sounding a little distressed.

"I know. It's dreadful that the school had no idea of what was happening on their very premises."

"What an ingenious idea her mum had, to use her shoe!"

These words were stirring a memory. A t-shirt with a skull on it, a sneering voice and a high-heeled shoe…

Her eyes snapped open. She was in a dimly lit room full of cosy beds. There was a lamp on a table next to her and a tray laden with food. To her other side were two people. A man with a long black beard, a bushy moustache and a round, cheerful face. The other was a caring looking woman with long, sweeping, blonde hair and a kind, caring face.

"Oh good. You're awake" she said. "Eat up. Eat up."

Megan sat up straight and immediately felt her head begin to throb unpleasantly. "Where's Emma?" she said automatically.

"Eat" repeated the woman firmly. "You are ever so pale"

Megan took a reluctant bite of toast, swallowed with great difficulty and tried to clamber out of bed, making the little man gasp and tell her to lie back down at once.

She ignored him. Unfortunately her recent bump on the head had made her feel strangely groggy and she swayed alarmingly.

Emma, she found out when she looked around, was lying in a bed to her right, apparently asleep, her face a sickly colour and her bedsheets pulled up to her chest.

Suddenly, she felt a hand close tight around her shoulder and push her forcefully back onto the bed, which she now realised was one of many in a small hospital ward.

The woman - who seemed to be a nurse - opened her mouth to say something but Megan got there first.

"Is Emma OK?"

"Just you concentrate on getting better" replied the nurse, firmly.

She sank back onto her pillows, feeling exhausted and took another small bite of toast, though she was not remotely hungry.

Over the next few days, Megan had many visitors, including her father and mother, who sat in the corner staring at her in a loving way. This was the first time in years her mother had taken the time to really notice her daughter and, though she did not speak, an understanding that they couldn't put into words passed between them in the times they made eye contact. Her father could do nothing but sob quietly, but Megan didn't mind.

***

A week later, Megan was discharged along with Emma, who was still slightly pale, which the nurses said was down to a lack of sunshine.

Grandpa came to see how Megan was doing, and mum and dad suggested that they go for a walk with Emma, and of course, they went straight to the sweet shop!

Her father told her a week later that St Brutus's had been put under the council's control, to cheers from Megan and Emma who were sitting eating the latest fudge.

The teachers, it transpired, were thieves in hiding and were now in prison, leaving the council to find new teachers who were capable of running a school with care and compassion.

The bullies were sent to a detention centre where it was rumoured they had to eat snails. Neither Megan nor Emma believed this but it didn't stop them wishing it were true.

Their life was back to normal, or as normal as it ever was. Even months later, Megan still remembered that remarkable week. The day she had made a friend, a friend for life. And a friend that she could go to the sweet shop with, whatever the weather!

About the Author

When Amy was 8, her class voted her 'Most likely to become an author' and the seed of a dream was sown. Now aged 11, she is really proud to be publishing this, her first book. Amy takes her inspiration from Judy Blume and JK Rowling and especially enjoys stories that tackle real issues for young people.

In her spare time, Amy enjoys Kung Fu and playing the clarinet as well as spending time with her twin sister, Cara, younger brother, Ross, and Ukrainian guest, Arevik.

Printed in Great Britain
by Amazon